Marijuana Leads To Murder

Teen Edition

By: Leonard McCaskill

I.S.B.N: 978-1456584726

Printed in the United States of America.

Preface

If you are reading this you must be in some kind of trouble. You are more than likely a teen who has been experimenting with pot, am I right? Also, you probably think Marijuana won't hurt your life. Well, let me tell you, you are 100% wrong.

How do I know? Well, I'm not some doctor or counselor. My experience comes from smoking pot at the age of 12, cocaine at 13, and then meth the same year. A lifetime of addiction that led to a prison sentence of Fourteen years for my first felony of manufacturing meth, and then to a life sentence for murder. Incidentally, my murder conviction is the only crime I am innocent of. Yes, I took a man's life, but it was during an attempted murder on my own life. We will get into that later.

Marijuana leads to murder does not mean if you smoke some pot you will go out and murder someone. What it means is marijuana is the gateway drug. It is the stepping-stone to harder drugs like cocaine, meth and heroin. And after a life of drug addiction you are in no position to go out and have the money to hire a real attorney when a murder case, like mine, comes along. All of this I will explain in this book.

This book is about the gateway drug marijuana.

Chapter 1
Introduction

My name is Leonard McCaskill. I am currently serving a life sentence for a murder conviction in Nevada State Prison. Which, by the end of this book, you will see is not a murder, but a self-defense case.

With that said, I take full responsibility for all my actions. Even though a lot of my actions came from peer pressure, I am responsible for every action I took, because, in the end, it is my choice. Just like every action you take is your choice.

Pot smoking, meth use, or cocaine use is a choice, a very bad choice, but never-the-less, a choice. And please take it from me, choose not to use now while it hasn't got a hold on you. If you think it won't get a hold of you, you are wrong, way wrong.

It's like this, the more you smoke pot, the more it will

call your name. At first you're thinking a joint every once in a while won't hurt you, but that joint will lead to a couple of joints a week, then to a joint every day. And if you're thinking a joint a day isn't a bad thing, it is. And if you are at the point of a joint every day, then look at what I just said in this paragraph. One joint every once in a while leads to a joint every day, or close to it. It's the stepping-stone to a drug addiction.

When I started using pot, I used to say all the time, "People who think pot is the gateway to harder drugs are crazy. Look at me, I don't use hard drugs." Have you ever said that? Well, within a year, I was using cocaine and meth.

This is how it happened to me.

I was smoking pot every day after starting with only a joint once in a while. Then, after becoming a full blown pothead in a year, someone had some lines of cocaine and I thought, "Well I use drugs every day I can handle some cocaine." Then, once I had used cocaine a half dozen times, some lines of meth came along. I thought I can handle it; I do hard drugs, so I did the meth. That led to a life of hell and drug addiction.

Please believe that pot was the stepping-stone to drug addiction for me and for 90% of people in prison. And for 99% of every drug addict in the world. Drug addiction does not start with meth or cocaine or heroin, it starts with pot.

Drug addiction starts with a bong hit, a pipe load and then a joint. Smoking pot takes the fear out of harder drugs. I pray that you are not that far along in your drug abuse. If you are, that gives you a trust in what I am saying, because I obviously know what I am saying.

I will throw this out there, if you have not used hard drugs yet, ask your parents or your counselor, or whomever you may be in trouble with, to take you to an NA meeting to talk with a lifelong drug addict. Or go to a drug program or the County jail to talk to a hard drug user and ask them if I am right.

I am right, but this is not about me, it's about you. If any one of these ideas helps you, then you're saved.

When I say the word saved, I mean your life. That is what we are fighting for, your life. Whatever your life is like now, you are so worth fighting for.

Here is the deal, where are you in your drug use? Are you experimenting with pot, a pot smoker, or worse? We can fix it. You just have to make the choice. And first off admit to yourself where you are with your pot use or drug use. That's our first step.

Once we figure out where you are with your pot / drug use, then we will figure out why you are using, but that is the next chapter.

So, where are you? Only you can be honest with yourself. You lie to yourself and it's over.

I know what you are going through, and hopefully, you don't like the feeling you get from pot, and you're doing it just from peer pressure. If I am right and it's peer pressure, that's the easiest to deal with. Just flat out change friends.

Within a short time of my pot use, I only surrounded myself with other kids who smoked pot. That was the end for me. I made the worst choice that I could have ever made when I was just starting to smoke pot.

I know peer pressure is hard to deal with. It really is. It truly is not fair. I know what you're going through. Talk to your parents, grandparents, aunts and uncles, brothers and sisters. If it's peer pressure, talk to someone.

Peer pressure was why I started smoking pot. I had no self-esteem so I thought I found a way to mask not having any. And what did it get me? I've had a lifetime of drug addiction, prison sentences and more mental pain than you can ever imagine. Drug addiction will take over your life so fast you will have spent your whole life in one kind of prison or another. Even when I was on the street (not in prison), I was still in a prison of drug addiction. Prison is prison.

It all started with pot!

There is a pattern. Let me ask you this; are you at a point where you are craving some pot? If yes, there's your pattern. Where do you think your cravings will go? There is only one place for them to go, up, up, up.

Chapter 2

Why Are You Smoking Pot?

- Peer pressure;

- Boredom;

- Low self-esteem;

- Loneliness;

- A bad home life;

- To piss your parent off?

- Because you like it?

Peer Pressure: Peer pressure is the worst thing about being a teen. You want to fit in. You want friends. And if you look up to someone and they are teasing you or putting pressure on you, the easiest way to not be embarrassed is to smoke the bong hit, or pipe load, or joint. I know what you are going through. It's a horrible feeling. No teen should ever have to experience that. Let me tell you, every teen goes through it. And not just drugs, there are a ton of peer pressure issues. As you well know!

One of the ways to deal with peer pressure, concerning pot or drugs, is to take your self out of that situation. I know it's the hardest thing you can think of. But, if you don't, you will end up a drug addict faster than you can ever imagine.

Listen, I know how it feels to be a teen with a pot problem, or just problems at all. It feels like a lifetime to only get through your teen years. Your teens are only seven years in a life that can last up to eighty or ninety years of age. But, those seven years can be the hardest, especially if pot / drug addiction is involved.

So, don't give into peer pressure. I know it's not that easy, but, you just have to take yourself out of the situation where pot or drugs are involved. And there is only one way to accomplish that: pick friends who don't use pot or drugs. It's that simple.

Make the choice that will change your life, and save your life. Your teens will be over so fast and your teens can shape your whole life, especially if things get out of hand with an addiction.

Boredom: Boredom is a cheap excuse, but it's real. It's a big reason for pot use or drug abuse. Being a teen can wear on you so bad and not all parents are very good with dealing with a teen's life.

Boredom is, sometimes, not a choice. If there is a money problem, boredom can be a real issue. I will be honest; this is a hard issue to deal with. Go to your parents, tell them! If they bought this book for you, you are a lucky teen, which means they care.

Also, if you believe in God get involved in a teen bible study, teen church group or a teen study group from your church, or a local church, even if you don't believe in God. Yes, some people might put peer pressure on you for that, but at least being in church groups won't ruin your life by making you into a drug addict.

If boredom is a trigger for pot use, do something about it. Anything! Something! Don't let boredom turn you into a drug addict. Can you imagine looking back over a horrible drug addicted life thinking, "I was only bored"?

Go to church. I didn't, I sure wish I would have. Church has the most activities and it is free.

Low self-esteem: Low self-esteem is horrible. You can have the most perfect home life and still have low self-esteem, let alone have a horrible home life. I have suffered from low self-esteem and lack of self-esteem all my life. And let me tell you, drugs overtook my life and I thought drugs helped. I was wrong, so very wrong. Why was I wrong? I spent a life deep in drug addiction and I still have low self-esteem. Now I choose to put my life in the Lord's hands and I am slowly building self-esteem. If the lord is not your thing, then go to your parents, councilor, or whomever you have to turn to.

I wish I had the answers for your self-esteem issues, but no one person will have the answers. But I will tell you this, pot; meth, cocaine or heroin is not the answer. If you let your self-esteem lead you to an addiction you will suffer from a self-esteem problem that you can't even imagine. You think you are in pain as a teen; you haven't got a clue how much pain an adult addict goes through.

Take peer pressure, boredom, low self-esteem, a horrible home life, loneliness and the worst heartbreak you can imagine and add that all together and you're not even close to being a drug addict. I wish I had the answers for self-esteem, unfortunately I don't. All I can say is this, don't try and compensate for low self-esteem with pot and drugs. Make a choice, stick to it!

Loneliness: is loneliness what pushes you towards pot and drugs? Loneliness is a painful feeling. Maybe at home your parents don't have time for you, or they work too much. Loneliness comes in lots of forms. No girlfriend or boyfriend is Another hard one. Your teens can be awkward, but let me tell you again, your teens only last for seven years. Don't let loneliness push you into a drug addiction.

There are ways to fight loneliness. First tell your parents. Then, if you have to, take your loneliness into your own hands by going to church, volunteer work, other family members, cousins, aunts and uncles.

The easiest way to become a drug addict is to find friends who use drugs, because they're lonely as well. And the biggest reason they will make you feel like your needed is that they need your money to go with theirs for drugs.

Don't let loneliness ruin your life. You want to know what loneliness is. I have already done thirteen years in prison, eleven of them for drugs alone. Loneliness is years of never getting a hug, years sitting in a cell, reading a book. Years! Think of your bathroom. Can you imagine spending years in your bathroom? Years!

You don't know loneliness until you are a drug addict, and you're sitting in prison with a life sentence at the age of forty. All because I started smoking pot!

A Bad Home Life: I don't think I need to explain what a bad home life is to anyone. That would take a book by itself. Anyway, I will say this, if you are being abused at home, either physically or sexually, go to the police. If you can't, then go to a family member, an aunt or uncle. Someone! Anyone!

Listen to me, abused teens turn into the biggest drug addicts. I am one. I never went to the police or family members for help. I used drugs, drugs and more drugs. And believe me; it did not make things better. It made them worse, way worse, unbelievably worse!

Ok, let's just say you have a regular bad home life, and I'm not saying having a bad home life is not painful; it alone can ruin a young life. There are millions of teens who never recover from a bad home life, it not only turns teens into addicts, but alcoholics, over eaters and the list goes on.

It might not seem like it right now, but your bad home life will come to an end. Drug abuse can last a lifetime. I have known a thousand drug addicts in my life, personally. I know six who have given up the drug life. And the six went through a life of hell.

What I'm getting at is don't let a horrible home life turn you into an addict. You will have a whole life that is more horrible than what you are going through now. Believe me, drugs only make it worse. Every day you probably say, "Life has got to get better!" It will if you quit the pot or drugs, I promise you. Are you trying to piss your parents off? Think about this, you keep trying to piss your parents off by smoking pot. Next thing you know, the pot will be calling your name. It's that simple.

Parents are not worth becoming a drug addict just to piss them off. You want to piss your parents off, turn out better than they are. Show them up; go to church, get better grades, and plan on going to a college that graduating along will set you up for a life. Like Stanford. Anything, just quit smoking pot just to piss them off.

You want more attention from them, tell them, and don't smoke a joint. Come on, stop and think about this one. The chances of you turning into a full-blown drug addict if you keep using pot are 100%. Trust a drug addict when I say it isn't worth it. Put yourself in my shoes. Is turning out like me worth pissing your parent off? I'm not even going to answer that. Make the right choice here, you're smarter than that!

Because you like pot: This is not a joke. If you already enjoy pot it could be over with already. If you don't get into rehab, go to church, and most importantly of all: change friends. If a friend smokes pot, quit being friends; period.

If you already have a craving for pot that is a sign of a drug addict. And you should be scared. Being a drug addict is more than just using drugs. It's called a craving, a craving like you can't imagine. A drug addict likes nothing more than to get high. More than their family, a job (if they're lucky to have one), their spouse, their children and their freedom.

It all starts with pot. It all starts with a craving to smoke pot. If you fight the craving now, it will go always. If you don't the craving for pot and hard drugs will last a lifetime and consume your whole life.

The truth is this, if you don't take this serious, right now, your life will be over. Pot, drugs, alcohol will ruin your life.

Trust me. All I have ever known were drug addicts. Their quality of life is so low, so painful, and so full of hardship; they all have lived a life of hell.

I have never met a drug addict who did not go through a horrible life. I have never met a drug addict who has never been in jail. I have never known a drug addict to stay married. Listen, there are addicts who pretend to have it all, but their quality of life is truly horrible.

You have one chance to live a life free of the pain drug abuse brings. Forget everything else I have said and start thinking about prison, prison, prison, prison.

Chapter 3

Prison, Prison, Prison

This is a true story of a pot smoker.

I have a drug friend, George, who used to use pot and cocaine. He finally got off of the cocaine after it caused problems with his heart, but he continued to smoke pot every night after work. He actually kind of turned his life around. George's family has money; he ran a small warehouse for them in Northern California. He got remarried and had two girls. But, he continued to take half a dozen bong hits of pot every night after his little girls went to bed. He would not smoke pot during the weekends because he was a semi-professional poker payer. George's family lived in Reno, NV so he played in poker tournaments every other week. He and his dad were going to a three-day tournament in South Lake Tahoe starting on a Friday afternoon. Thursday night in Northern California, after his little girls went off to bed, he smoked on his bong, about six hits.

Then the next morning after he got his girls off to school he

kissed his wife and headed for South Lake Tahoe to meet his dad

for the poker tournament. George and his dad played for twelve

straight hours, from noon till midnight on Friday, same thing on

Saturday. That weekend he didn't smoke pot. He didn't even

bring any with him. On Sunday, George and his dad got

bumped out of the tournament early so George's mother drove

up from Reno for the night; they all had a nice dinner, and then

went to a show. The next morning, on Monday, George's mom

and dad were going to do a little shopping in South Lake Tahoe

then meet George at his sister's house in Reno. To this point

George has not smoked any pot since Thursday night. On his

way off Mount Rose, his radio station kept coming in and out.

He was reaching for the radio while he was going around a

corner when he hit a rock in the road and instantly got a flat that

made him swerve into the oncoming lane and hit a Honda Civic

head on. There was a witness to the fact that he did hit a rock in the road. Anyway, George broke his collarbone, and the seventy

year old married couple in the Honda Civic died on the spot.

The coroner even testified to the fact that if the seventy year old

couple were younger they probably would have survived. The

Highway Patrol gave George a breathalyzer test on the spot and

he passed 100%. It was an accident. George was released from

the hospital later that day after he gave them a blood test.

George was devastated after the accident. He sunk into a deep

depression, but after six weeks he went back to work. Four

months after the accident, George was at the warehouse when

the Sheriff showed up and arrested him for DUI Manslaughter

(Driving under the Influence). At the jail he learned that he had

T.H.C. in his system at the time of the accident. He was bailed

out on both counts of manslaughter. Then, he sold everything he

could and came up with Fifty thousand dollars and his dad added

another Fifty thousand for his legal fund. With that kind of

money he was able to hire the best attorney in Reno, if not all of

Nevada. George and his attorney were able to postpone the trial for eighteen months. It was ridiculous that the court was saying the pot he smoked on Thursday night caused the accident, three and half days later. The problem is, the law states that if you have twenty parts per million of T.H.C. in your blood you are impaired to drive. But, since George smoked every night, the level of T.H.C. had built up. It takes up to thirty days for T.H.C. to leave the blood. George had thirty-five parts per million of T.H.C. in his blood, but he was not impaired the day of the accident. The District Attorney offered a plea bargain of ten years for each death (twenty years in prison). George was forty-five years old. George and his attorney said no way, he was not impaired, and they were going to trial. With the best trial attorney money could buy, George was convicted by a jury because the law stated that if he had that much T.H.C. in his blood he had no legal right to be on the road. Two joints in one week will put you over the legal limit. Two joints! George received twenty years, plus twenty, that is forty years in prison. With George's age at forty-five and a forty year sentence, you do the math. Incidentally, George's family spent a ton of money on appeals. They appealed all the way to the U.S. Supreme Court to no avail. All because of some bong hits.

When I was eighteen years old, I had a friend, Steve, who just started college. Never did any kind of drugs in his life. At a Saturday barbeque we talked him into smoking pot with us all day long. The following day he was on his way to the mall and a seven-year-old boy, chasing a ball, ran out into the street, and he hit and killed him. Steve was devastated. After he did ten years in prison he could not get a job to save his life: also, he could not get a license to drive for quite a while. All of this was because he got high the day before the accident. Also, he got beat up every day in prison because he was known as a child killer. Can you imagine? I can't.

Prison, Prison, Prison

There are many forms of prison. I know this guy named Tom who I worked with paving roads. He was a pothead, then a meth addict for twenty years. He lost his wife and three kids to meth. The loss of his family was more than he could handle. So, he got off of meth. He still smoked an eighth of pot a week. After about five years he remarried and had a little boy. But he kept his pot smoking from his new wife. They had a mortgage on a home and were doing well. One day we were out on a job paving a road when a roller ran over Tom's foot, totally crushing it. It was a total accident. The accident crippled Tom for life. At the hospital they had to do a drug test for workman comp. See, in every state there is a law that states every accident on the job requires a drug test, and if there are drugs in a person's system then the company is not responsible for the hospital bills or paying the persons wage. So, of course, Tom had T.H.C. in his system. He accumulated two hundred thousand dollars in hospital bills; he was crippled and then was fired. Within six months he lost his new wife and little boy and his house. He now lives off nine hundred dollars in social security and lives with his mom in a two-bedroom apartment – all because he smoked pot. Now he is in a prison on the streets.

Chapter 4

Bad Friends

A true friend is not going to hand you a joint. I know you are young and you think I don't know what I am talking about, but after twenty-five years of drug addiction trust in what I say. I have been in prison for thirteen years all together now. You know how many letters I received from so called friends who use drugs? Two. And they were so high when they wrote them I couldn't even read them. Do you know how much moncy they sent me over the thirteen years? Not one dime, nothing.

I remember when I was thirteen years old and every Friday I got ten dollars for the weekend. I had this friend who would be right there for me, I thought. We would combine our money and go by twenty dollars worth of pot. I thought he was my best friend in the world. I just knew we would grow old being best friends. There was nothing that was ever going to change that. We were best friends for five months until I got in trouble and my weekend allowance got taken away. He was gone. I could not see him for what he was. I was young and naive about drug addict's ability to use other people. My best friend came back a month later when my weekend allowance was back. I thought he was truly my best friend. Well my best friend came back with a new drug, meth. We started right where we left off. I had already done half dozen lines of cocaine before the meth came, so it was on after that. Well, he was my drug addict best friend who only used me and everyone else in his life. It was less than six months before my best friend, who was three years older than me had me selling dope for him. How long were we best friends? Eighteen months.

I use to sell little amounts of drugs, but never enough to have pockets full of money. I always owed the drug dealers. I used to get everyone high, and oh how I had friends. I can still remember them to this day. I was out of pot and a so-called friend called me up and asked me if I had anything. I said no, but hopefully sometime later on. He said he had a joint and would meet me at the park. On my way to the park I was thinking how this kid was such a great friend to be there in my time of need. We smoked the joint and he said he had to go. I remember sitting there watching him walk away thinking now that's a true friend, came all the way here just to smoke a joint with me. Of course he could call me for a joint anytime after that, which he did, all the time. Let me ask you, was he trying to help me out, or was he just feeding his own addiction? Well, let me tell you, we never hung out after that and that was the only joint he smoked with me and I am embarrassed to say how many joints I smoked with him.

What I am getting at is that you really need to look at your friends. Friends will lead you into addiction faster than you can yourself. Friends come in a lot of different forms. There are the friends who always need money from you for drugs, or to go in on drugs. They'll be there for you in so many ways you'll think they are your true friends. Someone is harassing you, you need a ride, all those things you go through being a teen. You think that's a real friend? Quit using or having money or get busted and see where your friends are.

Then there's the friend who never has money or never puts money in on the drugs. They are always first to be there for you in any way they can that doesn't have money attached to it. You think they're great friends. They're only there for the drugs and if you really think about it you know this. How many friends do you know that have been arrested? How many got arrested by them? One out of ten gets arrested by them selves. That means nine of them got arrested with friends. Can you see where I am going with this? Friends who use drugs, or just have bad behavior, will come up with bad ideas. Almost everyone who is in this prison I am in, who committed robberies, burglaries or theft, committed their crime with someone else. Two drug addicts won't last long together before they get into trouble.

When I was twenty three years old, I met this guy who cooked meth. I thought he was the best out of all my friends that I had. He was twenty years older than me. He had a bad ass house and hot rod cars. He took me under his wing and asked me if he taught me how to cook meth would I cook it for him. Oh yes, yes, yes, yes. I thought at the time, there couldn't be a better friend in the whole world. He was going to hand me my career, meth cook. Of course he did. In six short months I was a better meth cook than he was. Then six short months later we got busted for manufacturing meth. What kind of a friend was he? He told on me and he got probation. I got fourteen years for my first felony and I never heard from him again. No money, no letters, no nothing. He went back to cooking meth.

You have got to watch out for friends. Life is hard enough on you without adding a drug addict friend. A drug addict friend will only turn you into a drug addict. Then they will run you into the ground. Have you ever heard the saying, "Till the wheels fall off"? Well a drug addict made that up and it means until everything goes bad. Not till the end. As soon as things go bad, you're out of money or your drug connect gets busted, or killed, or the most occurring ... you get busted, then the wheels are gone, there're gone, period. You have probably already come across bad friends. You might not have thought of them like this before, but hopefully this will open your eyes.

Listen, you have a chance I never had. If you are reading this book you already have someone who cares. Whoever is making you read this is trying to save your life, not just punish you. You are only really punishing yourself. You have to realize if you keep surrounding yourself with so called friends who smoke pot, or worse, you will be punishing yourself. If you are reading this there is already a problem of pot in your life. Your parents, or counselor, or whoever is concerned for your future, already you have someone who will support you in your battle to get off of pot, or harder drugs. I would have given anything for someone to have cared when I was a teen.

Back to bad friends. Your friend who comes to you

behind your parents back to either get you high or to get high is not a true friend. There is just a drug addict who needs other people to feed their addiction. Some of you are thinking I am crazy because your best friend who gets you high without ever taking money from you or any car rides or whatever, they just are there for you to get high. Yes, there are friends who do that, I use to be one of them. Now that makes you the one using them. You are now the bad friend. Also, they are a horrible friend for feeding you addiction. A lot of the time, your friends are not trying to ruin your life by turning you into a drug addict. They just don't want friends who don't use. Just like you won't want anyone around you who doesn't smoke pot very soon, if not already. It's simple, if your life is all about smoking pot, you don't want some friend who does not smoke pot, giving you a hard time for smoking. That makes you a very bad friend. And you don't want that, do you?

There is one place that you can find good clean friends ever time, Church. Church has so many different programs that are fun and helpful for teens. If you already belong to a church and they don't offer programs, tell your parents you need to find a church that offers more for teens. Teen church groups will provide great friends. You can't go wrong with church. I have prison friends who tell me they grew up in teen church groups and never experienced drugs until they left the groups or grew out of them and did not continue with the church. If church is not part of your life, or you're not willing to go to church (maybe it is not in your upbringing), there are many ways to find other kinds of programs, such as the Boys and Girls Club, Boy and Girl Scouts or the D.A.R.E. program. Tell the counselor there your problems and needs.

Also, there is volunteer work. Volunteer for senior citizens or disabled people who can't do yard work. There is a lot you can do to change your life, so that you are not bored and drawn back to friends who use pot or hard drugs.

Please beware of friends who don't use pot or any hard drugs, but are trying to get you to use ecstasy. That is a big epidemic right now. Everyone thinks it's only a pill. Teens think if it's a pill it can't be that bad for you. Teens are under the impression that only large companies can make pills so they can't be all that bad. Well, let me tell you. I can go online and purchase a pill press and make my own pills just as easy as I can make lunch. Ecstasy is just large-scale dope cooking in other countries that like to exploit teens in our Country. So, run, run, run from any friends who talk about ecstasy. Ecstasy is the new generation drug that has irreversible effects on your nervous system, not to mention your heart. Irreversible effect!

Don't be a bad friend and stay away from bad friends. Even the ones who are not trying to be bad friends, they just don't understand.

Chapter 5

Why you must quit now before you turn 18

Remember, your teens only last seven years. I know that seems like a lifetime to you right now. But I promise you, once your teens are over life flies by and if you are a drug addict your problems only grow into a twenty four hour day, seven days a week job that is so mind and body controlling you have no idea. Eighteen years old means you can now do whatever you want with few interruptions. Yes, your family will be down on you for your drug use, but you will end up doing just like I did at eighteen. I just stepped away from my family. And now my mom won't have anything to do with me.

Once you're eighteen you can hide from the disappointments you cause your family and if you are an addict you will run with the addiction like never before. Very few people ever recover from drug abuse at the age of eighteen. You must take the craving away now. Your life depends on it.

I am really concerned about this chapter; I don't want to put thoughts in your head about turning eighteen and the ease of drug use once you're an adult. But that's my point exactly. Right now you have pressure to fight your cravings. Pressure from family, counselors, maybe even the law. Later on you will have a lot less pressure because you will be an adult. Don't get me wrong, it's not all fun and games being an adult drug addict. There is pressure from everywhere, because you are an adult drug addict. You will forever have problems paying rent or even keeping a place to rent. Drug addicts and car payments don't work well together. Power bills, water bills any bills will cause pressure for an adult addict. The problem is that it's very easy for an adult addict to hide from the pressure of these problems because even though they are horrible problems, who can really tell you what to do? No one. Yes, hopefully your family will share their disappointment with you in the hope that it will help you quit the drugs. Most of the time families give up after a period of time dealing with a loved one's drug addiction. Even though a family should never give up on someone, sometimes they have to because of finances or the adult drug addict (you in the future) is too destructive to the well being of a family. I promise you if you don't quit using pot and or heavy drugs now while you are a teen, your life will spiral into a life only painful drug addiction that will drain the life out of you, your family and loved ones. Believe me, it is easier to quit now before pot knows your name. Once it starts calling your name, it could all be over. If it's calling your name already, you must do everything there is to change your life right now before life as you know it and your family's life is gone forever.

The bottom line is family, counselors, or the law is now holding you back from becoming a time consuming, lifelong drug addict. Just think what will happen once all of these deterrents are no longer there to hold you back from a life of drug addiction. Right now is the time to do whatever it takes to change your life. Change your friends. Change your habits. Do whatever you have to do. Just do it. You have your whole life in front of you. Life truly starts at adulthood. Remember your teens only last seven years. Those seven years should be a time of growth to send you into adulthood with the tools you need to live a full life, a happy life, a prosperous life. Your seven years of teens should not be drug induced years that send you into adulthood with cravings for pot, meth, cocaine or heroin. The growth that you need should not have an addiction with it.

And if you think pot does not have the ability to grow into an addiction of it self, not only are you wrong, you know you're wrong. I don't care how young you are, you know pot is a drug. We all use to say or have said pot is not a drug, even though the law says it's a drug, the courts say it's a drug, socicty says it's a drug, church, our parents and doctors say it's a drug. Therefore, it's a drug. And no matter what anyone else tells you, you know pot is or can be a big problem. I could not do homework or schoolwork stoned. Can you? I bet you can't, not at a capacity that is a passing grade. Hopefully you are planning to go to college. You can't be a pothead and get a good education. You can barely get through high school, if at all, stoned on pot. Think about your future. I know, I know that is so far away, you think. But it truly is just right around the corner. You must seize the moment and quit using before you are an adult or else you will be an adult drug addict with no barriers to hold your addiction back.

Chapter 6

What drugs do to a family?

You have probably experienced what drugs can do to your family if you are reading this. Most of what I am about to write you probably already know. If you come from a loving family, drug addict family members will devastate them for life. Your addiction can make your family go through hell right along with you. A loving family will go through life doing all they can do to keep from suffering themselves. They will go to the end of the earth to save you from your drug addiction. All the while trying to do whatever it takes so they're not in pain anymore, seeing you go through your painful addiction. A loving family will feel that in some way it's their fault that you are an addict. They will go through changes right along with you. You will cause pain your family does not deserve. Your family will go through financial downfalls because of rehab. A loving family will suffer through years and years of heartache caused by you. All their pain will come from your addiction. And I bet you already know this. In all reality, a loving family will suffer every one of your problems as a drug addict. Do you want that? Your family will be happy on the outside to see you, and help you, but on the inside they will be in turmoil. Their hopes and their dreams for you will be crushed. They will just keep on loving you and loving you through all the pain you put yourself through. Then, one day, they will give up on you in some way. Yes, they will still love you, but they will have no choice but to financially cut you off. Because of a lifetime of your abuse, not your drug abuse, but your abuse to your family. A drug addict will abuse his or her family without really trying to hurt them (some drug addicts try, or know they are hurting their family). Most addicts get so deep into their addiction they are really only concerned about themselves. You have a chance right now, to stop using before you cause yourself and your family a life of pain. Think about it. Do you really want to cause your family a lifetime of disappointments and life changing events that you being an addict will cause? It's time to take your life back, before it's too late, before you take the life out of your loving family.

Now, if you don't have a loving family you will be on your own so fast. This will save your family a lot of heartache, but then your drug addiction will go unchecked and that reason right there is why you have to quit right now while you can and it's not too late. When an addict's family just gives up on him the addict can use all the drugs he wants. You, the addict, will go through job after job with no consequences, beside your finances. You will go through apartment after apartment with no consequences. And it all starts with pot. Although your family is not a loving family, it will still cause some pain. But if your family does not stand by your then, more than likely, if you don't stop smoking pot, you will turn into the worst kind of addict. A drug addict who has no family or loved ones will have nothing to hold them back from using all the drugs they want.

And if you have no restraints, then you will turn into the worst kind of drug addict. Most of these kinds of drug addicts end up in one of two places, the morgue or prison!

It does not matter which of the two families you come from. It's devastating on both kinds of families. The families that disown you, it's hard on them to give up on a child. I don't condone family giving up on their loved ones, but they are just not capable of being a loving family. In the long run it's worse for you, which is why you have to take control of your own life now. Period! If you have a loving family then any action your drug abuse causes is going to affect your loved ones right along with you. So, your consequences affect them also.

The bottom line is drugs cause families and loved ones a lot of grief. It's hard on everyone who loves you. It's sad to see a loved one go through the stages of pain an addiction will bring. Your parents see their child grow into someone who can't deal with everyday life, sinking into a drug addiction. For parents there is no other pain worse than addiction except death of a child. And with drug addiction it's a slow, prolonged death.

You don't want to put your family or loved ones through that do you? It's not fair to them, just because you won't quit smoking pot as a teen. It truly can all stop right here, right now. Think of your family.

Chapter 7
Prison or Dead

I am in a prison with nine hundred guys. I have been doing my own surveys. I have literally talked with four hundred of them and I asked them one question: what was the first drug they did? 95% of them say marijuana. That's a big number.

Since I got my prison number (that's all I am anymore) in 1995, one hundred thousand prisoners have came through the Nevada prison system. I think I have known less than a dozen people who never used drugs. I have had hundreds of prison friends and I guarantee they all started with pot. 95% of all prisoners started with pot. That came from a study behind prison walls, not by some doctor or counselor. You keep using pot you have a 95% chance of ending up in prison. This is no joke! People who have used drugs go to prison or die.

How many drug dealers do I know who never went to jail

or prison. One. And he is a snitch. He sells out his customers to keep from going to prison. Can you imagine buying you drugs from someone who goes and gets busted after selling you drugs and he tells on you just so he can sell drugs the next day? That's what you have to look forward to. You keep using pot, you will go to prison. This has been my life for twenty-eight years now. Believe me when I say everyone I know who uses drugs goes to jail or prison. If you think jail is not so bad, think of it like this: you have a decent job, a car on payments and an apartment, then you go to jail for six months to a year for simple possession of drugs. You will lose your job, your car and your apartment just because you went to jail. Then, once you get out, what do you have? Nothing! You have to start over again. Who is going to hire you? You are known to have done jail time. Why take the chance? You can't even use your old job for a reference. Is it worth it?

Let's talk habitual criminal, or the tree strikes law. In every state there is one of these two laws. All it takes is three felonies of the same charge to get either one of these sentences. Three possession arrests and you are looking at twenty five years to life. Period! Let me clarify this, if you live a life of drugs you will go to prison many times. Once you get two or three prison sentences you can get twenty-five years to life in prison for just getting a felony. Society is not messing around with repeat offenders. Too many ex-felons are progressing with their crimes. So, now there are laws that lock repeat offenders up. Period!

Then there is parole. I'll be honest with you, I have done more years in prison on parole violations for getting high than the years for the crime. I don't personally know one person who sent to prison and never came back to prison. Think of that one. Look at it like this, if you are reading this book you are already in trouble. Do you really think you can get away with anything in the future?

Drugs will make an addict commit all kinds of crimes. 95% of everyone I have talked to in my prison study said they were on drugs or committed their crime for drugs. Every criminal, from shoplifters (a shoplifter can do prison time if they get caught three times), car theft, burglars, robbers, embezzlement, forgery to murder are on drugs or because of drugs. Think about it, if the 95% of prisoners never used drugs or quit smoking pot in the first place, they would never have ended up in prison.

If you continue to use pot you will end up in prison. The fact that all these prisoners got here by starting with pot does not lie.

This part of my life is very depressing. In my twenty-eight years of drug abuse and prison I have known thirty seven people who have died from overdose and either murdered or died in the commission of a crime. Thirty seven people, think about that number. Did you know you can snort a line of cocaine and die? One line of cocaine can cause an aneurism in your brain. And teens are prone to cocaine aneurisms. I want you to put this book down for a minute and think about what one line of cocaine can do to you, ok?

Most of the people I know who died of an overdose died from mixing drugs. They never thought the little amounts of meth, cocaine or heroin would kill them, but when they use more than one kind of drug in a day it ends up killing them.

The worst for me was a very close friend of mine who quit using hard drugs for five years, but continued to smoke pot every day. She got her life together as much as a pothead could. She stayed out of prison, got remarried, and worked hard at her minimum wage job as was very happy. She was at a wedding and there was some cocaine addicts she used to party with. She slipped away and snorted one small line of cocaine and died of an aneurism that night. Absolutely unfair! To this day I can't get over it. One little line of cocaine and she's gone forever. Why would she do cocaine after so long? She was an addict, and it called her name. Just like if you don't stop smoking pot, drugs will call your name. I know four guys and one girl who got out of prison and were dead by noon from a heroin overdose.

Can you imagine that? You get out of prison at 8:00 a.m. and your dead with a needle still in your arm by noon. Yuck!

Keep smoking pot and that can be you.

Let's talk about the people I know who didn't die of overdose but now have lifelong serious medical conditions. First of all it is in the hundreds; yes I said hundreds, of drug addicts who have contracted Hepatitis C. Doctors say a person with aids will live longer than a person with Hepatitis C. I literally know hundreds of addicts with Hepatitis C. Plus, the number of people in prison with HIV from drugs is unbelievable. There are some IV users who don't have a disease, but not many. Why, because eight of ten drug addicts turn into needle users. That ought to show you where your future lies.

Now, the three biggest health problems drugs cause are to your heart, kidneys and liver. I can't even count the people I know who finally quit using drugs because they're now on dialysis. Truly the number is too large to even remember. Can you imagine having your kidneys fail you because of drugs?

Drugs cause so many heart problems. There is a rumor that meth can't kill you or you can't overdose on meth. Well, let me tell you that's BS. Teens, especially, can have heart attacks on meth because their hearts are still growing. Teens can cause long term heart problems using meth. Cocaine causes heart disease. Just a couple of years of cocaine abuse can enlarge your heart. And an enlarged heart is bad. Then you get sclerosis of the liver because most drug addicts are alcoholics as well. Alcohol and hard drugs will give you sclerosis, almost guaranteed. And the big thing about sclerosis is if you quit for any amount of time, like going to prison, then once you start using again it can simply kill you all because of pot.

Also, there are an alarming number of long-term meth users getting cancer. Not to mention most meth addicts lose teeth.

Now back to death over drugs. I have known sixteen people who lost their lives for, or over, drugs. That is another number that is ridiculous. Six of them were murdered for their drugs. They were drug dealers or people who use large amounts of drugs. The most drugs any of them had was one ounce of crystal meth. My drug friend lost his life over $1,200 of crystal meth (I will tell you about him later on). I had another drug friend who was stabbed to death for his $50 of heroin he just bought. He had to get high that night. Can you imagine going out to get some drugs to party one night and you are killed for your drugs? I also know ten people who died during crimes committed for drugs or because drugs had them in a violent state of mind, including the life I took (and we will get to that later as well). Three of them died in-home burglaries, four of them died during robberies so they could go get drugs, and three were so out of their minds committing crimes on drugs they got killed in the process. That includes the life I took. He used to be one of my best drug friends. He was over ten times the legal limit on meth. He was so high I had to shoot him twice with a shotgun to stop him.

Pot smoking will turn you into a drug addict. Then to a life of prison, if you lucky enough not to die of an overdose or get killed. Period.

Chapter 8

My Story, The Start Of My Pot Use

When I was twelve, one of my mom's many boyfriends took me to a friend's house to play video games. They were smoking pot out of a bong. My mom's boyfriend sat me in front of a bag of pot and had me load the bong for them. I felt cool, o yeah, I was a part of something. So, they were busy playing and told me to hit the bong, I really felt cool. I didn't even care what the bong hit would do to me. And, of course, I coughed my ass off. The next weekend I was asked if I was going to the same guy's house to play video games. I was shocked, they wanted me to come. I was a part of something. Yes, I went and as soon as we got there I was set in front of the bong and told to keep it loaded. Wow! At the time, I didn't think it was peer pressure. I just thought they thought of me as one of them. After two weekends on bong hits, I was a pot smoker, I thought. Then I noticed one of the kids I hung out with; his mom smoked pot. I told him I smoked pot. He was so impressed he stole some pot from his mom and we went out back and smoked it in one of his mom's pipes. He told every one of his friends and next thing I knew they were all bringing me pot to figure out how to smoke it. I was the cool pothead (who really did not care for the high) in the neighborhood. My home life provided little, if no, attention. So now all these kids were giving me attention. How could I not accept this new attention? Next thing I knew the pot was calling my name. I craved it from the time I got out of school. Forget homework! I only went home to eat then I was gone, looking for pot. By this time hardly anyone was looking for me to show them how to smoke pot because I had already shown them. So now I have pot calling my name and no attention from all the kids, plus no free pot to smoke. Now I am thinking about pot all the time. Then came my best friend, he found out I got $10 every Friday and he came to me and talked me into putting my money with his and we would split a quarter ounce of rag weed every weekend. There were no more movies for me, no more pizza slices, no more slurpies, no more roller skating, nothing else. If I got a dollar, I was buying a bowl of pot. If I got $2, I was buying a joint. Then one day on the way to school, I finished a joint from the night before. That was the end of sobriety for me; I had turned into such a pothead in six months I couldn't think of anything but marijuana. How did I get there; a little peer pressure, a little neglect from home, then a craving. It's all a pattern. I take full responsibility for my addiction. Although my mom never once got mad at me for my drug abuse, she didn't care one way or the other. Therefore, I was able to run after my cravings. And let me tell you, I did! And my so called best friend was right there every Friday. I thought he was there for me, but he wasn't. It was only the $10. He was older than me and I thought he was the absolute coolest kid in the neighborhood. Even though we only hung out on Friday nights, at the time, I thought he was only there on Fridays to help me out. I knew he was too cool to hand out with me all weekend. So, I had my fat bag of pot, I went my way, he went his way. Well now that I had no money so I couldn't go to the movies or roller-skating with my friends who didn't waste their money on pot. So, all I could do was hang with other potheads. Soon, I only wanted to hang with other kids who smoked pot. Our entertainment was hanging in someone's backyard or the park stoned. If I hung out with someone who didn't smoke pot, I either didn't have any money to go to the movies, or whatever, or they looked down at me for smoking pot, so that was the last place I wanted to be. So, needless to say I surrounded myself with the same kind of person I was. Now at school I was thought of as a stoner, one of those people. It was embarrassing at first, but all I had to do was stay away from the normal kids. After all, I thought they weren't my friends. My only true friends smoked pot. Then one day one of my so called friends stole some cocaine from his uncle and they were snorting lines and offered me one. I thought to myself, well, I use pot all the time, so I can handle some cocaine. Well, over the next six months I snorted half dozen lines of cocaine. I never cared for the high, but I thought it was cool. And I was cool because I now could tell other kids I used cocaine also. So, at the age of thirteen, I was into drugs and I thought I would never have a problem with drugs because I have them under control. I was under control. I was so under control when my so called best friend in the world found out I got smart with my mom's boyfriend and got my allowance taken away he left, I had no way to get my weekend pot, I was in a panic. I had to go hang out with kids I really did not like. These kids were out stealing bikes, shop lifting, stealing from their parents or anyone. I have to admit, I was scared being around these kids. They were violent, but they smoked pot all day long, so I was right there. Can you see how innocently it all started? It was a pattern that grew into a pot addiction that took so many things from me. My schoolwork suffered. I never went to the movies or skating again. No pizza parties, nothing that cost me money that most teens would save up for.

I also missed out on my teens, those years can be fun.

It all started with a pattern of pot use. If you can't see a pattern in our drug use, you really have a problem. It's not too late for you. You have to make a choice. I promise you if you don't stop using pot right now you will turn into a drug addict who uses hard drugs. The biggest promise I can make to you is that you will live a life of pain, prison or even death if you don't quite smoking pot right now. Period!

Chapter 9

Meth

Once my allowance was back my so called best friend was there on Friday night, with a whole new drug. I put my $10 with his $10 and we got a half gram of meth. I was right there because, after all, I was into drugs. So, I went right into an addiction of meth that has lasted a lifetime. I still needed my pot every day and meth every weekend. I spent my money on meth now; I was in need of more drug money. Well, my so called best friend did a home burglary and I stole $500 in change. We wrapped all the change up and he went and bought a lot of pot and meth. So, now I sold pot and meth to all the kids in my neighborhood. I never made any money for skating or the movies, I only made little amounts for pot and meth. I was so addicted to pot I had to have it every day. So now I was out pushing pot and a little meth to all the kids who were getting their allowance. I am a horrible friend. Now there was no glamour in being a low level drug dealer. I was always in trouble with someone because I owed money for the drugs. I was so lost; I didn't know what to do with my life. There were no sports, no dances, no extra school activities, nothing but drug use and the activities that drugs bring. I was not into crimes other than drugs. I thought I was not like everyone else because I hung out where the drugs were and I worked selling drugs for my drugs. I was wrong about that because I was responsible for pushing drugs on all the kids who were out stealing for their drugs. The drug dealers who I sold drugs for would tell me they need a new VCR or car stereo and I would go tell kids what my request was. Then they would go commit a crime they were not planning to commit. But, to drug an addict, that gives them the chance to get drugs for a stolen VCR, or whatever, was too great of an opportunity. So I am just as responsible for the burglary as they were. And if you end up in the same situation, you will be responsible as well. Or, if you are the one with the drug connection and you are getting everyone their drugs, you'll be responsible for their crimes they commit for their drugs. I was all of the above and I was only thirteen.

Meth took over my whole life by the time I was fourteen. My so called best friend was not my friend at all by this time. I was left with a drug addiction to meth and pot, and no way to pay for them. At fourteen years old I became the middle man for almost everyone in my neighborhood. I didn't sell the drugs, I was the one everyone took their money to and I would go get the drugs for them. I would pocket half the pot or meth. Did I ever sell my drugs for extra cash? No way! I was a full-blown pothead and meth user. Meth took over so fast so hard. I was fourteen and the next thing I knew, I was in prison. Ok I jumped ahead; I was smoking a joint a couple of times a week, then every day, then all day long. Sound familiar? Then a line of meth came along, then it was a line every day, then one day someone asked me if I wanted to smoke some meth, I was fifteen, I said sure. I was scared to death but I smoked it anyway. I spent my days waiting for someone who needed drugs. I only went to school because I didn't want to get in trouble. My schoolwork and homework suffered badly. There was no graduation in my future.

Meth is a drug that will control you for life. Adults go downhill fast on meth. Just think what it will do to a teen. My teens were gone before I was out of my teens. The meth controlled me to where I wanted nothing to do with my family, nothing to do with family functions, BBQs, weddings, holidays, nothing; and I was only fifteen. Meth became my life before I had a life. I didn't even know what life was about, and incidentally, I never would. I still don't know it in all reality. I went from my teens to sitting in this prison cell with a life sentence and I never discovered what life was all about. I do know being a pothead and meth addict in my teens took away any chances at knowing what life could be once I turned into an adult. If you don't quit using pot and hard drugs now, while you can, you will not have the tools you need to go into adulthood and discover what life is all about. I promise you!

I became a drug addict in my teens. I never had the illusion that I would quit using drugs once I turned into an adult. That's how powerful an addiction will become. Once I cared about nothing except drugs, I knew my life would be drugs. And nothing could stop that: and nothing has stopped it, not even prison. Addiction is that powerful. More powerful than you parents, your pride, your self respect, your self-worth and most importantly your freedom. I know you are thinking how your freedom can be more important than your parent. Nothing is more important than your freedom. Why that is because your freedom means everything, it means how much your parents mean to you if you lose your freedom over drugs. You had to see it coming and so did your parents. Yet you still lose your freedom whether your parents' feelings get hurt or not. Freedom will take everything from you except your addiction. Nothing will ever take that from you. Your addiction will walk over your relationship with your parents. And if your parents can't stop your addiction, then your freedom won't mean anything to you at all.

You are probably thinking I'm talking about later in life. No, I am talking about your teens. Addiction in your teens will take your parents from you, your freedom and possibly your life. Even though meth and my drug addictions took over my whole life, I had it easy compared to some teens I knew. I had friends who were in juvenile hall the entire time they were a teen. I knew girls who sold their bodies for drugs, and ended up raped or pregnant or with a disease. You probably know some teens that are probably in bad shape like some of the teens I knew. Addiction is not prejudice. It will take over the teens that have a perfect home life, to the teens that have the worst home life. Pot will turn your life upside down so fast, that the next thing you'll know you're an addict; you have no family or freedom.

Ok, I just went off on a tangent, but it was a good tangent. It took me getting innocently convicted of murder and a life in prison to really understand what my life has meant. I sat back and thought how in the world did I waste my life on drugs? It all comes down to my teens, my early teens and pot. Actually, it started preteen with me, but by the time my teens started, I was an addict and this is how my life and everyone else's life will end up if they turn into an addict in their teens.

This was my future. What is your future?

Chapter 10

Adulthood

Drugs were my future. Why? Because being an addict during my teen age years became my education. The one thing you must do in your teens is go to school and get your education. If you are consumed with your addiction then you won't have time for school.

With me, when I was fifteen, sixteen and seventeen years old, my addiction took precedent to everything, including my education. By the time I was eighteen, I had been a drug addict longer than it takes to get a doctorate. I was a full blown addict at adulthood. And I knew nothing else. I did not care, I was going to live a life of drugs and now that I was eighteen no one was going to stop me. Not one, not even the law.

I quickly turned into a terrible drug dealer. I never made any money, I barely made more drugs. Even though I committed felony after felony every day selling drugs, I was never able to live the life I had always heard about. One out of every hundred drug dealers makes money for houses and cars. And those drug dealers end up in prison for life for drug trafficking. My drug dealing lasted for a while but I struggled to pay my rent, and I was lucky if I had a car. I was also hungry a lot. Believe me it's nothing like on TV. Being eighteen and nineteen is a blur to me. I went from apartment to apartment, paranoid that I had too much traffic. I had girlfriend after girlfriend, who just wanted me for my drugs. So I thought I would find a girlfriend who did not use drugs. I found a girl who smoked pot but did not do hard drugs. What was I thinking, drugs are drugs. This relationship turned out to be one of my worst relationships in a long line of bad relationships.

Pot is a drug. Don't ever think it isn't.

I only had two short jobs in two years, both at minimum wage because I could not pass a drug test for a better job. I could go without meth long enough to pass a test. However, pot takes a month to get out of your system and I could not go a

month without smoking pot. Even though I was a meth addict,

pot still controlled my life. If you even think pot doesn't control

your life you are wrong, way wrong. When you an addict you

don't realize how much drugs control you. I used to say, I'm in

control of my drug use. It's the other way around. Drugs

controlled me. By the time I hit my twenties I quit selling meth

so I could sell pot instead. I thought my life was finally turning

around. Of course it didn't, I had more traffic and more

problems than ever. So I moved away to Arizona to get away

from all the drugs and guess what happened? There were more

drugs in Arizona that I had ever seen before. I was right in the

mix so fast that two years blew past faster than I could ever

imagine. Did I have any fun? Not one day! Did I make any

money? I went back to California broke after two years of a

drug induced coma. I went to Arizona in a car, and left on the

bus. Don't go thinking Arizona was one big party, because it

wasn't. Yes, I got high, but it was nonstop problem after

problem.

Drug addiction is not fun. It's a twenty-four hour a day job that will consume your life. You can never keep anything for very long. Not a job, car, relationship, place to live, friends, food, drug connections and most important, your freedom.

The bottom line is that drug addiction: pot, meth, cocaine, heroin and even prescription pain pills will run you all over the state or country. You will go where the drugs are. Instead of going where family or a job takes you. You will go where the drugs take you. If you don't think drugs can run your life like this you are crazy. You have no future except prison and/or death using drugs. When I moved back to California, I decided the best place for me was with an uncle of mine who used drugs. It was a new town with the same addiction. By the time I was twenty two years old, I was destined for prison or

Death. I was such a drug addict nothing mattered except drugs, nothing. I had turned into a go-no-where, do nothing drug addict who cared for nothing or no one except myself and my habit. And if you think I was alone in my addiction, you're wrong. There were many, many other addicts who where just as miserable in their abuse. I never even saw where I was heading or where I had come from at twenty-two I would have never guessed my whole life would go wrong because I started smoking pot ten years before. My whole miserable waste of a life is because I smoked pot when I was twelve and kept on smoking pot. Now at the age of twenty-two what was left of my life was just about to blow up in my face. With in two years my freedom would be gone for life.

Chapter 11
Dope Cooking

When I was twenty-two I moved to Reno to get away from my drug life. I moved to my aunt's house. I knew no one at all. I was going to start all over, no drugs. Well, within a week I met some girls who used meth and I was in. I was strung out on meth within a month. It took me no time at all to find a good meth connection. Once of these guys was cooking meth. We became close friends. He was twenty-five years older than me. He offered to show me how to cook meth, I said, "Hell yes"! So he took me under his wing, but he would only show me the end process. Once he could see I would be good at it he stopped showing me and had me selling meth for him. For once I was making enough money to rent a house and I got a truck. But that didn't last long because I discovered a new addiction, gambling. After six months this guy could see I was trust worthy and he made a deal with me. If he showed me the whole process of cooking meth, would I cook the meth and only sell it to him? Of course, he taught me the dirty deed and I became better than him in six months. For the first time in my life, I had money. I was spending it all in the casinos, but I had money. I had a new girlfriend every other week. I thought I finally hit the big time. The guy who hooked me up was getting all my drugs for half of what they were worth, and I was paying for all the chemicals to make the meth. But he was my best friend. After all, he hooked me up with my new career. This went on for a year. I was twenty four now and I only sold my meth to my best friend. I was very loyal. I was making a lot of money, but he was getting rich. Then one day I moved my lab to a new spot because my best friend needed extra meth that weekend, which I thought was weird, but who was I to complain. So I set my whole meth lab up and while I am cooking the meth, the cops raided me. I could not believe I got busted. I was not on the street selling meth. I only sold it o one person. How could this happen. I knew my best friend would not sell me out. Well, I was so wrong. My so called best friend got busted and told the cops he would give up his connection and since it was the person manufacturing the meth in exchange for probation. He got caught with enough meth that he was facing a mandatory prison sentence of ten to twenty five years in the Nevada Prison System. I spent over a year in the county jail fighting for my life. The only thing that saved my life was that I had no record. So I took a plea bargain of fourteen years in the Nevada State Prison. My so-called best friend got six months probation and was cooking meth within a month after I was in prison. He would get busted and get probation four more times before he went to prison for kidnapping.

Now, I was in prison on and off for the next eleven years. I finally expired my fourteen years in 2006. In eleven years I had one year and seven months out of prison. I did more time on parole violations for dirty UAs on meth than I did for the crime of manufacturing. For the life of me I could not stay clean. I would use meth even knowing one dirty test would send me back to prison. Why? Because a drug addict does not care about freedom, family or friends. A drug addict only cares about themselves.

Don't think it's all easy to get high and forget your problems. Because it's not! Your problems will eat at you all day and all night. You'll get high and worry about everything. Are you going back to prison tomorrow? Will you be able to pay your rent? Will your family ever talk to you again? It's a never ending misery.

85% of every person in prison will come back on a parole violation for getting high! Listen, drugs will rule your life in more ways than you can imagine. It is truly a miserable life being a drug addict. And I can honestly say, out of the thousands of drug addicts I have known, none of them are happy, none. Drugs consume your relationships in a horrible way. On drugs you are never rational. You will lose relationship after relationship over going back to prison, over getting high.

Smoking pot will lead to drug dealing, dope cooking and prison or death. Being a drug addict you will only have drug addict friends. So, just like me, you won't have a chance if and when you get parole.

Once I got out after four years and I had a choice, go to my cousins house who never did drugs or go to a friends who used drugs. Where do you think I went? I chose to go to my drug addict friend's house. I walked in and he gave me a hug and bag of meth that had me back in prison a month later for a dirty drug test.

It's that easy to throw your life away over getting high. If you go back to smoking pot after reading this book or your done being in trouble with your parents your life will be over, that easy. I promise you, you will end up with your own version of my life. Period!

You will end up in prison or dead.

Chapter 12

The Things Prison Took From Me

Besides the obvious, my freedom, prison has taken my family members from me. I have this aunt I call Sis because growing up we were as close as brother and sister. I lived with her many times. I moved to Reno to get away from my drug life in California, so when I got arrested for manufacturing meth she was right there for me, money, phone calls, visits and most important mental support. After years of my drug abuse and parole violations, she rightfully got tired of being there for me. Then we had a falling out and I did not talk to her for quite a while. It absolutely breaks my heart that she is not in my life. She was more of a mom to me than my own mom was. For her not to be a part of my life is unbearable. When I got arrested for this existing murder case, we started talking again. Then, from my past prison sentences and parole violations she got tired of the pattern of my past and got the total wrong idea about my case and said some things that hurt me so bad. A lot of it was true about my past. I am an innocent man in prison and will die in prison. But because of my past, my family does not want to help me because there're tired of me being in prison. I am going to die in prison because my family is fed up with me. If I had not wasted my life on drugs and in prison, I know my Sis would go to the end of the earth to get me free from this hell I am in. But not only will I never get out of this place, I have lost my Sis forever. Even though I know I can writer her, I can't because she has this perception of me now, adding to the rest of my miserable life, it is unbearable. I'm an innocent man whose favorite aunt thinks I am not worth fighting for. There isn't a more painful family situation like this, like in my life. All because I kept smoking.

All six times I have gone to prison, three prison sentences and three parole violations , I have lost the girlfriend I was with. Two of them, I could have made my wife. I loved them so much. To this day, I still hurt over them. Four of them were good girls. That's six relationships that I was in love, they were in love with me. But the second the handcuffed were on, it was over with them. Yes, it took a while, but they all went elsewhere. Here is the unbelievable part; every one of them never broke up with me. They all just quit answering the phone, quit writing, sending money. They all broke it off by ignoring me till I quit trying. Can you imagine being in a cell knowing your girlfriend or boyfriend now loves someone else because you are locked up, because you never stopped smoking pot? When I am on the streets, I'm the one all the girls want to be with. I know that sounds conceited, but once I get locked up, I am forgotten, period.

The murder case I am serving time for is not over drugs like you would think. It has nothing to do with a drug addict's life. I started dating a girl who had a sick stalker ex-boyfriend who came after me to kill me. Next thing I know her ex-boyfriend and his best friend where after us. I ended up killing

76

his best friend, which I will get into soon. Anyway, I end up getting convicted of murder and the girl ignores me now. We are through, but she won't even tell me why. I have lost my life all over a girl I started dating and now she won't talk to me because I am in prison. She, of all people, knows I am innocent and still she won't help me get my freedom. I am all alone and I am innocent. Innocent people go to prison all the time. They usually have friends and family who fight for them. I have no one.

Prison will take more from you than you even knew you had. Plus, it will take everything you know you have. Prison is more than just your freedom; prison is the loneliest place on earth. If you think you are lonely now, wait till you are in a cell somewhere and you have no one to call. I mean no one at all. I lost the girl I am in love with because I am in prison. It was her ex-boyfriend tried to kill me. Try to figure that one out, I can't.

Every so called friend I had I have lost. If you can put yourself in my place, think of your life, every one of your friends, family members, girl or boyfriend just quits having anything to do with you.

I got a life sentence and I never got one letter from anyone saying, "hang in there" or "we are sorry your there". When you go to prison they put you in an intake unit where you are locked down twenty four hours a day for six weeks. No books, no anything but a shower every other day. You do get mail. I spent six weeks in a cell without one letter from family members, friends or my girlfriend. Try that on for size.

I am a good person; I just have worn my family and friends out with me always being in prison. And now that I need them the most, I am truly on my own.

Material possessions can be replaced. Friends, family and girl or boyfriends can't. But I have lost everything I own four times. I mean everything. The first time I went to prison I lost a Harley Davidson, a Ford 4X4, and my quads, plus all my furniture, all my clothes, all my pictures, absolutely everything I owned.

Imagine your parent's house. One day you go out somewhere and you get arrested and you lose everything in your house, everything from the clothes to the dishes. Then it happens three more times in your life. Every time I got out of prison I had nothing period! It's just how it is. All your possessions become someone else's, from your clothes to your girl.

Prison takes everything from you.

Chapter 13

What Led Up To The Day
I Took A Life?

I started to date this girl. She was totally the wrong girl to date. She had an ex-boyfriend who challenged all her boyfriends. We really hit it off, we were inseparable. I knew about her ex-boyfriend, Rodney, but I was blind to what could really happen. Rodney ran around with one of the meanest, one bad man who walked the streets, Todd. Rodney was a big bad-ass himself. So they caught me alone one day and they beat the crap out of me, black eyes, cuts but I healed up in a couple of days. So I thought it was over. My girlfriend and I went on living our lives for a short time. I was living at Bret's, my old landlord, shop that had a studio in the back. We ran around having a good time, not worried about Rodney because I had already been beaten up for being with her. Was this girl the one

I wanted to marry and have kids with? No! not at all. She was fun and we needed each other at the time. So, we went on living life for about two months. One day, we went to get diapers for a friend. While I was inside the store, I ran into the Todd who helped beat me up. As soon as he saw me he was after me. As I was leaving the store Rodney came in after me. My girl was outside in the car; she had the car ready to get out of there. The two guys chased me out to the car saying they were going to kill me. They chased us for a while but we got away. We just thought they were drunk or just being angry. We went about living, when Bret called me and told me they just came to the shop. They suckered Bret out of the shop, slapped him around and said they were coming after my girlfriend and I . Now I had enough, I was worried for my girl. I am not one to call the cops so I really was scared. I never thought they would really kill me. They were so big and good at fighting ,why try and kill me when they can just beat me up. So all that day I was really trying to figure out what to do, after all, I am not a coward. The last thing I wanted was for these guys to catch us and really hurt us. I have a friend, Sam, who is as big as them. I went and asked Sam if he would come with me while I fought them so all this BS would stop. The crime I committed to this day was a misdemeanor for fighting. I went to the shop and call them to come over and fight for the girl. I would take an ass whipping because I knew I could not whip them.

The night I took a life

Rodney and Todd showed up at 11:30pm and Rodney came out of the truck like a bull. The second I started to fight back he went into a rage and started yelling he was going to kill me. He ran back to Todd's truck and Todd handed him a baseball bat. I started to run as Rodney was chasing me saying he's going to kill me. Well, as I am running I tripped and fell to the ground and he was on me, he hit me in the forehead, I don't remember anything after the first hit. Bret is the star prosecutions witness in my murder trial. He testified that Rodney stood over me beating me in the head saying, "Your dead mother Fucker" over and over. When the prosecutor asked

Bret how many times Rodney hit me in the head with the bat,

Bret said, "Until Rodney got tired." The whole time I am

begging for my life, remarkably I never lost total consciousness.

I was out on my feet. I don't remember any of this. The star

witness said at this point I was bleeding profusely from my head.

I had a four inch gash across my forehead and the back of my

head was split in five different places. The whole time my

friend, Sam, is trying to get to me to stop Rodney from killing

me, but Todd is preventing him from stopping Rodney. Sam

finally gets Todd to take the bat from Rodney by threatening

Todd with a digging bar. As Todd took the bat out of Rodney's

hand it gave me a split second to stumble into the shop. The star

witness said I ran into the shop and held the door shut. Rodney

came over to the door and overpowered me and pulled the door

open and came in after me. Well, I ended up so scared for my

life after being hit in the head more times than anyone could

count, that I grabbed Bret's shot gun he kept for protection and

as soon as Rodney saw I had a gun he ran out the door. Again, I

don't remember any of this. The star witness said that I came out the door covered in blood and shot Todd, who was holding

the bat in his left hand. I shot Todd in the chest from five feet

away and he never went down. Then I shot him again to put him

down. I kind of came to after the second shot with the shot gun

in my hand. I was in so much shock I ran to my truck and

somehow, I was able to drive off.

Is this pre-meditated murder?

I took a man's life; I now have to deal with that for the

rest of my life. And, to be honest, it's hard to deal with. So,

because of my record and I fled from the scene, I got arrested for

murder with a deadly weapon. I was so beat up from the

baseball bat, I now have scars for life, my speech is impaired

and my motor skills are affected. I'm sitting in jail assigned a

public defender. The public defender advises me this is a self

defense case all the way around, the very worst case scenario, a

manslaughter case. I can live with a manslaughter charge, even

though they were teamed up to kill me. Now, here is one of the

many unbelievable things of the case. Rodney is never charged for standing over me repeating he is going to kill me while he beat me repeatedly in the head with a bat. Although I am charged with murder for shooting Rodney's friend, Rodney is free of charges. He is never even arrested. So after six months I get a new lawyer the court appoints me. I am happy; I just know this guy is going to bust his ass for me. Well, I was wrong. My new attorney's investigator did absolutely nothing. There were five people Rodney had beaten with baseball bats in the past. But Rodney would never get charged. My new investigator refused to investigate any of these people and he refused to get any 911 calls with Rodney's name in them. By the time the trial came my attorney was such a horrible attorney I was screwed. Then when we were picking the jury, there was a man in the jury pool who was an attorney and played softball on the same softball team with the prosecutor in my case. My attorney left him in the jury pool and he ended up on the jury and became the jury foreman. The trial was a joke from day one. The witness to the shooting said I was about to die from the baseball bat. The last blow to my head and the first shot was about thirty seconds.

Well, the jury came back after two hours with a guilty verdict of murder with a deadly weapon. Then I got sentenced to life in prison, plus five to fifteen years for the weapon enhancement. Now here is where the title of this book comes in. Marijuana was the gateway drug to a life of drug abuse. Then a lifetime of prison sentences led to a true self-defense case. If I had assets at the age of thirty-seven I could have hired a real attorney and I would not be here, or at least I would have a parole date from manslaughter charges.

Chapter 14

Finally The End

    I hope you can see a pattern in my life. I never thought my life would end up like this. All because I started smoking pot. Yes, I lived a life of drugs, but do I deserve to be in prison for life? I don't think so and there are a lot of people who think I got a raw deal. I sit in my prison cell about to turn forty. The girl this was all over has nothing to do with me. If I do get out it will be in my late sixties. My father is sixty years old now I will more than likely lose him while I am in her. My mother won't write or visit. My favorite aunt won't fight for my freedom. I have never been married and I have no kids. I get to appeal but the court keeps appointing me attorneys who are worthless. I can't even explain how lonely I am. My chest is on fire twenty four seven. I have already done thirteen years in prison all together and I can't get over my emotions. I am so out of my mind with pain it's a wonder I was able to write this book. I hope this book can open your eyes to what pot can lead to.

And prison is filled with worst-case scenarios.

The bottom line is what are you going to do with your pot or drug use? Do you want to end up like me or half as bad as me? Even half as bad as my life turned out is pretty bad. My life has been so full of misery and it won't be changing any time soon. All because of drugs! Yes, my murder conviction had nothing to do with drugs, but in the end it was all about a lifetime of drug abuse. I can't stress the fact that pot is the gateway drug to all other drugs: meth, cocaine and heroin. You have got to see this. Pot will lead you down a road of addiction that will last a lifetime. That's providing you're not killed or die of an overdose. The night I was beat with a baseball bat I drove to a drug friend's house where my girl was at. He was a descent friend, generous, would help in any way possible. Anyway, I drove to his house all beaten and bloody scared to death, it would be the last time I saw him. He would be dead in four months over one ounce of meth. He was robbed at gun point and after the person got the meth, he shot him just for the hell of it. It was a needless killing, the robber had the drugs. The cops refused to spend any man hours on my friend's death because he was nothing but a drug dealer. There were two girls in the apartment who witnessed the robbery. The cops absolutely refused to do anything about the robbery. You could end up just like this, you get killed the cops don't care because you are a drug addict. I guarantee my friend started with pot.

Pot is a vicious circle; it starts with pot and then goes who knows where. It won't be good, I promise you.

You should hopefully be able to see a pattern in your life. I pray you can see this and change your future right now. No more pot or any drugs. Just make a choice to live a life free of drugs.

I will end with this. Church is the one for sure place to find friends who don't use drugs. Church is a place of God. If you live your life for the lord you won't let him down or your parents. Most importantly, you won't let yourself down. The lord will give you a place of refuge from pot and drugs. You can't go wrong with church. Please just try it, if not for yourself, for your parents. If you parents bought this book for you to read, believe it or not, they truly do care about you. You have a lot more of a chance than I ever had.

www.ingramcontent.com/pod-product-compliance
Lightning Source LLC
Chambersburg PA
CBHW030405290526
45785CB00004B/1905